The Dictionary of Received Ideas

GUSTAVE FLAUBERT

For Mark Olsen

With Best Wishes

from

Geoffrey Wall

The Dictionary of Received Ideas

GUSTAVE FLAUBERT

Translated by GEOFFREY WALL
Preface by JULIAN BARNES

SYRENS

GUSTAVE FLAUBERT 1821–1880

SYRENS Published by the Penguin Group. Penguin Books Ltd, 27 Wrights Lane, London W8 5TZ, England. Penguin Books USA Inc., 375 Hudson Street, New York, New York 10014, USA. Penguin Books Australia Ltd, Ringwood, Victoria, Australia. Penguin Books Canada Ltd, 10 Alcorn Avenue, Toronto, Ontario, Canada M4V 3B2. Penguin Books (NZ) Ltd, 182–190 Wairau Road, Auckland 10, New Zealand. Penguin Books Ltd, Registered Offices: Harmondsworth, Middlesex, England. Published in Syrens 1994. Translation copyright © Geoffrey Wall, 1994. Preface copyright © Julian Barnes, 1994. All rights reserved.
Set in 9.5/12pt Monotype Bembo by Datix International Limited, Bungay, Suffolk. Printed and bound by Page Bros., Norwich.

PREFACE

Accepted idea, received idea, fashionable banality.

Bouvard et Pécuchet, Flaubert's last novel, left unfinished when he died in 1880 and published the following year. The story of two clerks who set off to understand and master the world. They fail in everything, and return in the end to what they know best: copying.

Copie. Flaubert's plan was that after the events of the novel were complete, he would add a second volume. This would consist of the 'Copie' of the two clerks: a vast mass of curious and exemplarily stupid material, which would include the Dictionary of Received Ideas.

Du Camp, Maxime. Flaubert's friend, who tells us in his memoirs that the Dictionary had been one of the novelist's earliest projects: one he was talking about when he was twenty. By the time it is first mentioned in Flaubert's Correspondence – in a letter to Louis Bouilhet from Damascus in 1850 – it is already a well formed idea.

Erection. Two years after his letter to Bouilhet, Flaubert gives a fuller description of the project to Louise Colet. It would begin with a grand, tongue-in-cheek preface, 'the historical glorification of everything generally approved'. Then would come the Dictionary: 'It would include, in alphabetical order and covering all possible subjects, "everything one should say if one is to be considered a decent and likeable member of society".' He sends Louise half a dozen sample entries. Among these is Erection, whose definition does not change over the subsequent thirty years.

Flaubert, Gustave. Born Rouen 1821, died Croisset 1880. A genius.

Genius. 'No point in admiring *genius*, it's a "neurosis".'

Human Stupidity. Flaubert said of *Bouvard et Pécu-*

chet that 'It could have as its subtitle "The Encyclopedia of Human Stupidity". This undertaking gets me down and my subject becomes part of me.' Though he was close to vomiting when at work on the poisoning scene in *Madame Bovary*, no manifest diminution of intelligence has been recorded while he was writing *Bouvard et Pécuchet*.

Irony. The Dictionary is one of the most ironical works ever written: it is the world placed in Flaubert's press and squeezed until the pure oil of irony runs out.

John Bull. 'When an Englishman's name is not known, he is called John Bull.' The Dictionary was first published in France in 1913, thirty-three years after Flaubert's death. John Bull waited another forty-one before translating it into English in 1954. It has been virtually out of print ever since.

Knowledge. Always to be distinguished from wisdom; never more so than in the present work.

Laporte, Edmond. Flaubert's friend, who helped him with the vast task of preparing and sorting the 'Copie', including the Dictionary.

Manuscript. The manuscript of the Dictionary is a mess. It exists in two forms, with no indication of a final state; and quite a number of the definitions are not even in Flaubert's own hand, but in that of Laporte. (Were they dictated by Flaubert to Laporte, or written by Laporte and put up for Flaubert's approval?) Finally, though some of Flaubert's definitions have been crossed out in the manuscript with his own hand, these deletions continue to be printed in modern editions of the Dictionary: such is the greed, love and disobedient curiosity of Flaubertistes.

Number. The more people who believe in an idea, the less likely it is to be true: see the prefatory maxim from Chamfort. Is this the case?

Oil. Flaubert was once travelling on a train when a stranger asked him: 'Don't you come from So-and-so and aren't you a traveller in oil?' 'No,' replied Flaubert, 'in vinegar.'

Pyramid. 'Useless edifice.' Flaubert once compared a work of art to a pyramid: it stands in the desert, magnificently useless; jackals climb to the top of it and bourgeois piss on the base of it. The Dictionary is a small pyramid which took a whole writing life to cut and dress.

Quiche. See: Satire.

Railway. In Flaubert's eyes, a symbol of stupidity, as well as a promoter and distributor of the same. The railway is stupid, what people say about it is stupid, what people say on it is stupid. See: Oil.

Satire. One way for the writer to confront the stupidity of the age; the other being irony. The satirist wheels the world onto the stage, throws custard pies at it, pulls down its trousers, mocks its paunch. The ironist wheels the world onto the stage and offers it slices of quiche, praises its fashionable plus-fours, observes that embonpoint is the sign of a truly serious person.

Thirteen at dinner. Always to be avoided, as Flaubert notes in the Dictionary. After his funeral in Rouen in 1880, a group of literary mourners sat down to dinner. The poet Théodore de Banville counted heads, and right-thinkingly insisted that the streets be scoured for a fourteenth diner. Eventually a private on leave was persuaded to join the funeral party. The soldier had never heard of Flaubert, but came because he was keen to meet the poet François Coppée.

Ultraviolet. To put it another way, the ironist takes

over at the end of the satirist's spectrum. The satirist can manage a splendid, dramatic, indignant indigo. But there are colours beyond indigo. Violet, which melts into ultraviolet: the shade of the ironist, the shade the world cannot see.

Visibility. Central to Flaubert's aesthetic was the invisibility of the writer. In the Dictionary, as generally in the Copie, he achieves the maximum of invisibility. His authorial absence is so complete that you could almost say he didn't write the work, that the Dictionary is the product of others. Flaubert just listened.

Wilde, Oscar. Said: 'Flaubert is my master.' And on another occasion: 'Flaubert did not write French prose, but the prose of a great artist who happened to be French.'

X-ray. See: Ultraviolet.

Yes-men (and women). Flaubert targets not just vacuities of social form but also the mindlessness of packaged thinking. Today he would be listing the grotesqueries of political and linguistic correctness. An American newspaper recently produced a stylebook discouraging use of the word 'normal' in describing a person, as this implied that other human beings might be . . . abnormal. The offstage noise is of Flaubert laughing.

Zzzzzzzzzz. Is it possible to read the Dictionary straight through? No: you would fall asleep. Do not mistake it for a book of wisdom. It is not La Rochefoucauld. It's one of those books you might pick up when in a state of exasperation with the world, read a few entries, and put it down, consoled that a finer and more exasperated mind than yours had passed this way before. It might even be the sort of book that works while remaining on the shelf. You just need to think about it, its stance and technique, for a rueful smile to appear on your lips, and for the Dictionary to have done its job.

Julian Barnes

TRANSLATOR'S NOTE

The translation is based on the much-augmented text of the *Dictionnaire des idées reçues* presented in Geneviève Bollème's edition of *Le second volume de Bouvard et Pécuchet* (Paris, Denoël, 1966).

With thanks to all who generously helped me along with advice, encouragement, and inspiring conversation: Joe Bristow, Gianna Chadwick, Malachi Chadwick, Hugh Haughton, Nicole Ward Jouve, David Moody, Sara Perren, John Roe and Susan Tealby.

Geoffrey Wall

The Dictionary of Received Ideas

Vox populi, vox Dei
> Proverbial

'I wager that every public notion, every received orthodoxy is a piece of foolish nonsense, since such great numbers have found it to their taste.'
> Chamfort, *Maxims*[1]

A

ABROAD Enthusiasm for everything foreign, sign of progressive thinking. Contempt for everything un-French, sign of patriotism.

ABSINTHE Exceedingly violent poison: one glass and you're dead. Journalists drink it while writing their articles. Has killed more soldiers than the Bedouins. Will be the destruction of the French Army.

ACADÉMIE FRANÇAISE Denigrate it, but become a member if you can.

ACCIDENT Always 'deplorable' or 'unfortunate'; as though anyone might find some cause to rejoice in misfortune.

ACHILLES Add 'the fleet of foot'; everyone will think that you have read Homer.

ACTRESSES The ruin of respectable young men. Are appallingly lubricious, frequently engage in orgies, squander millions, end up in the workhouse. Excuse me! some are excellent mothers.

ADMIRAL Always gallant. They swear by saying: 'Jumping Jelly-fish!'

AGE, THE PRESENT AGE Denounce vigorously. Lament its unpoetic tone. Call it 'an age of transition, of decadence'.

AGENT Obscene word.

ALABASTER Used to describe the most beautiful parts of a woman's body.

ALCOHOLISM Cause of all modern ailments. (See *absinthe* and *tobacco*.)

AMBITION Always described as 'insane' except when it is 'noble'.

AMBITIOUS In the provinces, any man who causes comment. 'I'm not an ambitious man!' means selfish or incompetent.

AMERICA Fine example of injustice: it was Columbus who discovered it and it's named after Amerigo Vespucci. But for the discovery of America we would not have had syphilis or phylloxera. Praise it to the skies anyway, especially if you've never been there. Deliver a tirade on *self-government*.

ANDROCLES Mention Androcles and his lion when the conversation comes round to animal-taming.

ANGEL Impressive word in love and in literature.

ANGER Stirs up the blood; healthy to lose your temper once in a while.

ANIMALS If only they could talk! Some of them are more intelligent than humans.

ANTICHRIST Voltaire, Renan . . .

ANTIQUES Always forgeries.

ANTIQUITY *And everything to do with it*, clichéd and boring.

APLOMB Always 'diabolical' or 'superb'.

ARCHITECTS All imbeciles. Always forget to include the staircase.

ARISTOCRACY Treat with contempt, regard with envy.

ARMY The bulwark of society.

ART Leads to the workhouse. The arts are quite useless because they are being replaced by machines which can do the job better and more quickly.

ARTISTS All hoaxers. Extol their disinterestedness (*old-fashioned*). Be amazed that they dress like everyone else (*old-fashioned*). Earn insane sums of money, but it slips through their fingers. Often invited out to dinner. Woman artist must be a whore. What artists do can scarcely be called work.

ASP Creature found in Cleopatra's basket of figs.

ASSASSIN Always 'cowardly', even when intrepid and audacious. Less culpable than an arsonist.

ATHEISTS Any nation of atheists would surely die out.

AUTHOR Advisable to 'know a few authors'; no need to remember their names.

B

BACHELORS Always selfish and given to debauchery. Ought to be taxed. Destined to a lonely old age.

BACK A thump on the back can give you tuberculosis.

BALDNESS Always premature, caused by youthful indiscretions, or the gestation of great thoughts.

BALLOONS One day, men will go to the moon in a

balloon. It has not yet been discovered how to steer them.

BANDITS Always ferocious.

BANKERS All rich. Sharks and skinflints.

BANQUETS Always a most genuinely convivial occasion. Everyone is so sincerely reluctant to leave that they always arrange to meet again at the same time next year. A wag must say: 'At life's rich banquet, a hapless guest . . .'[1] Reform banquet always veal and salad; various kinds of banquet, to be elaborated: military, academic, old boys', birthday.

BASILICA Grandiose synonym for church. Always imposing.

BATTLE Always bloody. There are always two victors: the winner and the loser.

BEARD Sign of virility. Large beards cause baldness. Good for protecting cravats. Various styles.

BEAUTY SPOT Good place for writing poetry.

BEDROOM In an old château. Inevitably, Henri IV once slept there.

BEDROOM, BACHELOR'S Always untidy, with women's whatsits left lying around. Smell of

---

[1] Quotation from *Adieux à la vie*, an anthology piece by Nicholas-Joseph Gilbert (1751–1780), a minor satirist. The next line reads: 'One day I appeared, and then I died.'

cigarettes. There must be some bizarre things hidden away in there.

BEER Don't drink beer, *it'll give you a cold.*

BEETHOVEN Do not pronounce it Beet-oven. Swoon nevertheless when someone plays one of his works. 'What harmonies!' Praise the *legato.*

BEGGING Ought to be forbidden, yet never is.

BELGIANS Refer to Belgians as counterfeit Frenchmen; it always raises a smile – 'Did you realize. . .'

BELLOWS Avoid using them.

BELLY Say 'abdomen' when ladies are present.

BIBLE The most ancient book in the world.

BILL Always too high.

BILLIARDS A noble game. Indispensable in the country.

BIRD Yearn to be one, and say with a sigh: 'Oh for a pair of wings!' Indicates a poetic soul.

BLACK PUDDING Sign of domestic revelry. Indispensable on Christmas Eve.

BLONDES Randier than brunettes. (See *brunettes.*) Blondes always look good in blue.

BLUE-STOCKING Scornful term designating any woman interested in matters intellectual. Quote Molière in support: 'Our fathers, on this point, were very sensible, that a woman always knows enough as long as her mind rises to the level of knowing a doublet from a pair of breeches.'[2]

BODY If we knew how our bodies were made we would not dare to move an inch.

BOILED BEEF Healthy stuff. Inseparable from the word *carrots*: boiled beef and carrots.

BOOK Whatever it is, it's too long.

BOOTS On very hot days never forget to mention policemen's boots and postmen's shoes. Allowed only in the country, in the open. Only in boots does one feel properly equipped.

BOWER Very moving word. Works well in a poem.

BREAD People have no idea of the muck they put in it.

BREATH To have bad breath lends an air of distinction. Avoid any allusion to 'flies' and insist that it comes from your stomach.

BRONZE Metal of classical antiquity.

BRUNETTES Randier than blondes. (See *blondes*.)

BUDDHISM 'Bogus religion from India'. (So defined in Bouillet's Dictionary, first edition.)[3]

BUDGET Is never balanced.

---

[2] From *Les Femmes savantes*, 1672.

[3] Nicolas Bouillet (1798–1864) was the author of a notoriously superficial and inaccurate *Universal Dictionary of History and Geography* which circulated with the special approval of the University of Paris.

BUGGER To be used only as a swear word, if at all. (See *doctor*.)

BURIAL All too often premature. Tell stories of corpses that devour their own arms to stave off hunger. Do not let yourself be confounded by those who say that asphyxia takes care of everything.

BUTCHERS Frightful in times of revolution. All butchers are plump. Invariably brutish, always knocking children over in the street.

C

CABAL Sound indignant as you say it.

CACHET Always preceded by 'a certain'. It has a certain cachet.

CAMEL Has two humps and the dromedary only one. Or else the camel has one hump and the dromedary has two. (Everyone gets confused.) To be as sober as a camel.

CANDOUR Always charming. People are either totally candid or utterly lacking in candour.

CANNABIS Not to be confused with cannelloni, which produces no sensation of voluptuous ecstasy whatever.

CANNON-FIRE Affects the weather.

CANNONBALL The breeze from a cannonball can make you go blind.

CARBUNCLE See *pimples*.

CARIBOU So called because they come from the Caribbean.

CARRIAGE Express nostalgia for the days of the horse-drawn carriage.

CARTHUSIANS Spend their time making Chartreuse, digging their own graves and saying to each other 'In life we are in death.'

CATHARSIS Only used to refer to 'the experience of tragedy'.

CATHOLICISM Has been an excellent influence on the arts.

CATS Treacherous creatures. Call them salon tigers. Cut off their tails to prevent vertigo.

CATS AND DOGS When you see a black cloud approaching, you must say: 'It's going to rain cats and dogs.'

CAVALRY More aristocratic than the infantry.

CAVES Usually inhabited by thieves. Always full of snakes.

CELEBRITIES Unearth the minutiae of their private lives so that you can denigrate them. Musset was a drunkard. Balzac was up to his eyes in debt. Hugo was an old miser.

CENSORSHIP Has its uses, whatever people may say.

CHAMBER-MAIDS Prettier than their mistresses. Know all their secrets and betray them. Always deflowered by the son of the family.

CHAMPAGNE Distinctive feature of a formal dinner. Pretend to loathe it and say: 'It's not really wine.' Occasion for great enthusiasm among the lower orders. 'They drink more champagne in Russia than they do in France.' French ideas have spread all across Europe because of champagne. In the Regency period, people did nothing else but drink champagne. You don't drink it, you 'knock it back'.

CHARCUTERIE Anecdote about the pâté made with human flesh. Always a pretty woman to be found behind the counter.

CHARLATAN Always described as 'odious'.

CHATEAUBRIAND Known principally for the steak called after him.

CHESS, GAME OF Simulates military tactics. All the great generals were good chess-players. Too serious for a game, too frivolous for a science.

CHIAROSCURO No one knows what it means.

CHILBLAINS Sign of good health. Caused by warming up too quickly.

CHILDREN Flaunt a lyrical affection for them, when in company.

CHIMNEY Always smoking. Topic in any conversation about heating systems.

CHOLERA Eating melons gives you cholera. Cure it by drinking large quantities of tea laced with rum.

CHRISTIANITY Freed the slaves.

CHURCH TOWER (IN VILLAGE) Makes the heart beat faster.

CIDER Spoils your teeth.

CIGARS The ones you buy over the counter are 'all foul'. The only decent ones have been smuggled in.

CITY FATHERS Denounce loudly over the state of the roads. 'What do our city fathers think they're playing at?'

CLARINET Playing the clarinet causes blindness: all blind people play the clarinet.

CLASSICS, THE One is supposed to know them.

CLIMAX Rhetorical term.

CLOGS Rich men who started out with nothing were always wearing clogs on the day they arrived in Paris.

CLOWNS Have their joints dislocated in early childhood.

CLUB Always belong to a club. Conservatives get

[11]

angry about them. Fussy conversation about the correct pronunciation.

COAST-GUARD Never use this expression in the plural when referring to a woman's breasts.

COFFEE No good unless it comes through Le Havre. The best is a mix of Martinique and Bourbon. Coffee makes you witty. After a big dinner party, drink it standing up. Very *chic* to take it without sugar. People will think you must have lived somewhere out East.

COGNAC Deadly. Excellent for various ailments. A nice glass of cognac never hurt anyone. Taken before breakfast, kills tapeworms.

COITUS, COPULATION Words to avoid. Say: 'Intimacy took place . . .'

COLD Healthier than warmth.

COLLEGE More impressive than a school.

COLONIES (OUR) Mention them in a sad tone.

COMB, LARGE-TOOTHED Makes the hair fall out.

COMEDY In verse, not appropriate to the modern age. Even so, high comedy is not to be dismissed. *Castigat ridendo mores.*

COMETS Express scorn for people who used to dread them.

COMFORT Splendid modern discovery.

COMMERCE Conversation on the theme of which is the more illustrious, commerce or industry?

COMMUNION First communion: the greatest day of your life.

COMPETITION The soul of commerce.

COMPOSITION At school, composition tests your stamina, whereas translation requires intelligence. But in later life you can scoff at those who did well in composition.

CONCERT-GOING Respectable pastime.

CONCESSIONS Never make any. They were the undoing of Louis XVI.

CONCUPISCENCE Word used by a priest to mean carnal desire.

CONFECTIONERS Everyone in Rouen is a confectioner.

CONFINEMENT Word to avoid; replace with 'happy event'. 'When are you expecting the happy event?'

CONGRATULATIONS Always 'sincere', 'hasty', 'heartfelt'.

CONSERVATIVE Any politician with a pot-belly. 'You narrow-minded conservative!' 'Indeed I am sir. Only the narrow mind can keep us on the straight path.'

CONSERVATOIRE Essential to be a subscriber to the Conservatoire.

CONSPIRATORS Always have a mania for writing down lists of their own names.

CONSTIPATION Influence on political convictions. All men of letters are constipated.

CONTRALTO No one knows what it means.

CONVERSATION Politics and religion should be excluded.

CONVICTS Always look the part. All very clever with their hands. There are men of genius in our prisons.

COOKING In restaurants: always causes constipation. Home cooking: always wholesome. Mediterranean cooking: too spicy or far too oily. Beef broth: avoid if not home-made.

COPAIBA OIL Pretend not to know what it's for.

CORN ON THE FOOT Better than a barometer for indicating a change in the weather. Very dangerous when badly cut; quote examples of horrible accidents. Avoid climbing stairs, it gives you corns.

CORSETS Hinder conception.

COSMETICS Ruin the skin.

COSSACKS Eat tallow candles.

COTTON WOOL Especially useful in the ears. Basis of all social life in the Lower Seine region.

COUNTRY Country people better than town dwellers: envy them. In the country almost anything is acceptable: shabby clothes, practical jokes, etc.

COUSIN Advise husbands to beware of any young men their wives refer to as 'my little cousin'.

CRAYFISH Walk backwards. Always refer to reactionaries as 'crayfish'.

CREOLE Spends the day in her hammock.

CRIMINAL Always 'loathsome'.

CROCODILE Imitates a baby crying to lure people to it. Do not pronounce it *cocodrile*. The skin is superb for making gloves. Crocodile tears.

CROSSBOW Splendid opportunity to tell the story of William Tell.

CRUCIFIX Looks nice above a bed and at the guillotine.

CRUSADES Benefited the economy of Venice.

CUCKOLD Every woman has a duty to cuckold her husband.

CUDGEL More lethal than the sword.

CURLS Unmanly.

CUSTOMS DUTIES Express indignation and avoid paying them.

CYMBAL Always 'clashing'.

CYPRESS Tree that only grows in cemeteries.

CZAR Pronounced Tsar, and sometimes 'Autocrat'.

D

DAGUERROTYPE Will replace painting. (See *photo-graphy*.)

DAMAGES Always sue for.

DAMASCUS Only place where they know how to make swords. Decent blades all come from Damascus.

DANCE What they call dancing these days is just walking up and down.

DANCING-GIRL[4] Phrase that inflames the imagination. All women in the Orient are dancing-girls. (See *odalisques*.)

DANUBE Turkish Rubicon.

DARWIN The man who says we are all descended from a monkey.

DAYS Monsieur has his special days, such as beard day, doctor's day, and so on. Madame has her days too, at certain times of the month, which she calls 'particular'.

DEBAUCHERY Source of all ailments suffered by old bachelors.

---

[4] The word is *bayadère*, derived from the Portuguese word *balladeiras*, meaning *dancing-girl*, and one of the key words in a diffuse mid-nineteenth century fantasy of Oriental eroticism.

DECONTAMINATION Disagree over the pronunciation of the word.

DECORUM Impressive. Casts its spell over the masses. 'Decorum must never be sacrificed!'

DEICIDE Denounce it, even though the crime is so rare.

DELIGHT In poetry: phrases expressive of.

DEPUTY Great honour to be one. Denounce the Chamber of Deputies. Too many windbags. All layabouts.

DERBY Racing term. Very chic.

DESCARTES *Cogito, ergo sum.*

DESERT Image of the infinite. Produces dates.

DESSERT Gaiety. Keenest pleasure there is. Express regret at the fact that people don't sing over dessert these days. The virtuous will express their scorn for it: 'Goodness me! Cakes! No, I never indulge!'

DEVIL Used only in the expression 'It's quite devilishly cold!'

DIAMONDS One day we shall discover how to make them! And to think they're only coal! If we came across one in its natural state, we wouldn't even bother to pick it up!

DIANA Goddess of chase-titty.

DICTIONARY Exclaim: 'Only for the illiterate!' A

rhyming dictionary? I'd be ashamed to use anything of the sort!

DILETTANTE Rich man, keen on opera.

DIMPLES Always tell a pretty girl that cupids are
nestling in her dimples.

DIPLOMA Sign of knowledge. Proves nothing.

DIPLOMACY Splendid career, but exceedingly difficult and mysterious. Only suitable for aristocrats.
Rather vaguely defined profession, but superior
to commerce. Diplomats are always subtle and
penetrating.

DIRECTORY Scandalous period of history. 'In those
days men of honour had taken refuge in the army.'
Women, in Paris, walked the streets naked.

DISORDERLY HOUSE Highly organized.

DISSECTION An outrage upon the dignity of the
dead.

DIVA A female opera-singer must be referred to as a
diva.

DIVORCE If Napoleon had not divorced Josephine,
he would still be on the throne.

DOCTOR Always refer to him as 'the good doctor',
and, in informal masculine conversation, use the
exclamation *bugger me*. Thus: 'Well, bugger me,
doctor!' A genius when you trust him, a complete
idiot once you fall out. All materialists. 'The

thing is, they can't find our souls with their scalpels.'

DOCUMENTS Documents are always of the greatest importance. Every conspirator ever arrested has been carrying compromising documents.

DOG Specially created to save its master's life. The dog is a man's best friend because he is his devoted slave. Put sulphur in their drinking water to prevent rabies. To express a bitch's milk use a ring of wine-corks.

DOLMEN Something to do with ancient Gaul. Stone used for druid sacrifices. Found only in Brittany. Nothing further is known about them.

DOLPHIN Carries children on its back.

DOME Architectural form of tower. Express some surprise that it stays up on its own. Mention two: the dome of Les Invalides in Paris, and that of St Peter's in Rome.

DOMINOES Best played when tipsy.

DORMITORIES, SCHOOL Always 'spacious' and 'well-ventilated'. Preferable to single rooms, for moral reasons.

DOUBT Worse than negation.

DRUNK Always preceded by the word 'roaring'.

DUEL Denounce loudly. No proof of courage. Prestige of the man who has fought a duel. If you get a scratch, keep your arm in a sling for as long as possible.

DUNGEONS Inspire gloomy thoughts. The straw is always damp. Appalling places. No one has yet discovered a pleasant dungeon.

E

EARLY RISING Sign of morality. If you go to bed at four in the morning and get up at eight then you are lazy. But if you go to bed at nine in the evening and get up at five the next morning, you are energetic.

EARTH Mention 'the four corners of the earth', since it is round.

ECZEMA Sign of good health. (See *pimples*.)

EDUCATION Always foster the impression that you are well-educated; the 'intelligent' classes find it impossible to imagine anything else. The common people don't need any education at all to make a living.

EGG Point of departure for a philosophical dissertation on the origins of life.

ELEPHANTS Renowned for their memories. Adore sunshine.

ÉMIGRÉS Earn their living by giving guitar lessons and making salads.

EMOTION Always inevitable when making one's debut.

EMPIRE 'The Empire brings Peace' (Napoleon III).

EMPRESSES Always beautiful.

ENAMEL We have lost the secret.

ENCRUSTED Only ever with reference to mother of pearl.

ENGLISH WOMEN Express surprise that they have such pretty children.

ENGLISHMEN All rich.

EPACE, GOLDEN NUMBER, DOMINICAL LETTER Found on calendars, no one knows what they are.

EPICURUS Declare your contempt for him.

ERADICATION Used only in relation to poverty or else 'natural heat'.

ERECTION Used only in referring to monuments.

ERUDITION Scorn it as the mark of a narrow mind.

ETRUSCAN Antique vases are all Etruscan.

ETYMOLOGY Nothing could be easier, with a bit of Latin and some careful thought.

EVACUATIONS Often 'copious' and always 'foul-smelling'.

EVIDENCE Right under your nose, until it leaps out at you.

EXASPERATION Invariably 'at its peak'.

EXCEPTION Say that it 'proves the rule'; do not offer to explain why.

EXECUTIONER Post handed down from father to son.

EXECUTIONS, PUBLIC Deplore the women who go to watch them.

EXHAUSTION Always premature.

EXHIBITION Source of wild excitement throughout the nineteenth century.

EXPIRE Only ever use the word in relation to newspaper subscriptions.

EXTIRPATE This verb is only used in relation to heresies and corns.

F

FACTORY Dangerous and unhealthy to have in the vicinity.

FALSE TEETH Call them 'My third teeth'. Beware of swallowing them in your sleep.

FAME Merely a puff of smoke.

FAMILY Always mention it in a respectful tone.

FANFARE Always 'resounding'.

FARM When you visit a farm you must eat only

brown bread and drink only milk. If eggs are served as well, exclaim 'Good God, how fresh they are! No chance of ever finding anything as good as this in town.'

FARMER Always call him: Squire So-and-so. All farmers are well off.

FAT Fat people don't need to learn how to swim. Drive executioners to despair because they are so difficult to put to death. E.g. Madame du Barry.[5]

FATE Exclusively romantic word. A 'man of fate' is one who has the evil eye; 'Offenbach is a man of fate.'

FATHER 'My late father . . .' as you take off your hat.

FATWA Refer to any authoritarian decree as a 'fatwa'. It annoys the government.

FAVOUR Children, you do them a favour by boxing their ears. Animals, you do them a favour by thrashing them. Servants, you do them a favour by sacking them. Scoundrels, you do them a favour by punishing them.

FEAR Lends wings.

[5] Marie Jeanne, Comtesse du Barry (1741–1793), formerly the mistress of Louis XV, had grown so fat by the time of her execution in 1793 that there was some difficulty in getting the guillotine to do its work.

FEET Smelly feet are a sign of good health.

FELICITY Always perfect. 'Your cook is called Felicity, well then she must be perfect.'

FEMALE A word only applied to animals. In contrast to the human race, the females of animal species are less beautiful than the male. Quote various examples: the pheasant, the cock, the lion.

FENCING Fencing masters know secret thrusts.

FEUDALISM Have only the vaguest idea of what it is, but denounce it loudly.

FEVER Sign of being full-blooded. Caused by plums, melons, April sunshine, etc.

FICTION, IN SERIAL FORM Cause of demoralization. Argue about probable endings. Write to the author with your own suggestions. Outrage when you discover a character with your name. Novels published in serial form have a much more positive moral effect upon the reader than novels published in hardback. (See *novels*.)

FIG LEAF In sculpture, an emblem of virility.

FIGARO, THE MARRIAGE OF One of the many causes of the French Revolution.

FIRING-SQUAD More noble method of execution than the guillotine. Delight of the person granted this privilege.

FLAG, THE NATIONAL A sight to make the heart beat faster.

FLAGRANTE DELICTO Phrase used only in relation to cases of adultery.

FLIES *As flies to wanton boys . . .*

FOETUS Any anatomical specimen preserved in alcohol.

FOOD In boarding schools the food is always 'wholesome and abundant'.

FOREHEAD Wide and balding, sign of genius or self-assurance.

FORGERS Always work in cellars.

FORKS Should always be made of silver, they're much safer. Best to hold it in your left hand, it's easier and it looks more distinguished.

FOSSIL Proof of the flood. Tasteful joke, when alluding to a member of the Academy.

FOUNDATIONS, OF SOCIETY I.e property, family, religion, respect for authority. Invoke angrily if they are being undermined.

FRANCOPHOBE Use this expression whenever referring to German journalists.

FREE TRADE Cause of all economic problems.

FREEMASONRY One of the many causes of the French Revolution. The initiation ceremonies are terrible. Men have died as a result. Causes argument between husband and wife. The church does not approve of it. 'What on earth is their secret?'

FRESCOES No one paints frescoes these days.

FRICASSÉE You can only get a decent fricassée in the country.

FROG Female toad.

FRONTISPIECE Excellent place for engraved portraits of great men.

FUCHSIA Pronounced *few-shuh*.

FUGUE You have no idea what it is, but you should assert that it is extremely difficult and very boring.

FULMINATE Splendid verb.

FUNDS, SECRET Enormous sums of money which goverment ministers use to silence people. Denounce loudly.

FUNERAL 'Just think, I had dinner with the man only a week ago. Who would have known?' (said while following the hearse). Called obsequies in the case of a general, interment in the case of a philosopher.

FUNNY At every possible opportunity you must say: 'That's funny!'

FUR Sign of wealth.

FURNITURE Cherish it fondly. Always be anxious about your furniture.

FUSILLADE Only way to silence the inhabitants of Paris.

G

GAIETY Always 'frantic'.

GAME No good unless left to hang.

GAMES 'Innocent' games; what they are. Society games. Games and laughter. Express indignation at this 'fatal addiction'. Serious games: whist, chess. Vulgar games: picquet, écarté, bezique. Club games: lansquenet, baccarat. Café games: dominoes, backgammon. Silly games: draughts, pairs. Noble games: billiards.

GARDENS, ENGLISH More natural than French gardens.

GARLIC Kills intestinal worms and provokes erotic skirmishings. They rubbed it on Henri IV's lips the moment he was born.

GARRET Splendid place to live when you're twenty!

GARRISON Schoolboy garrison: headlice. Student garrison: pubic lice.

GARTER Garters must always be worn *above* the knee by women of fashion, *below* the knee by women of the working class. A woman must never neglect this sartorial nicety, there are so many insolent men on the streets these days.

GENIUS No point in admiring genius, it's a 'neurosis'.

GENOA In conversation with a tourist who is talking about his trip to Genoa always say, 'D'ya-know-a little place in Genoa?'

GENTLEMEN Extinct species.

GERM Germs of an idea. Inculcate the germs. Germs of the passions.

GERMANS Race of dreamers (*old-fashioned*). No wonder they beat us, we weren't ready!

GIAOUR Fierce expression, meaning unknown, thought to be connected with the Orient.

GIBBERISH What foreigners speak. Always scoff at any foreigner who tries to speak your language.

GIFT Don't value the gift by its price. Prize the gift for its value. 'It's the thought that counts.'

GIRAFFE Polite word to be used when you wish to avoid calling a woman a cow.

GLOBE Tasteful word to use when referring to a woman's breasts. 'Please allow me to kiss your adorable globes.'

GLORIA Always most consoling.[6]

---

[6] *Gloria* may mean either the hymn beginning *Gloria in excelsis Deo*, or it may mean coffee with whisky in it.

GLOVES Lend an air of respectability.

GOBELINS A Gobelins tapestry is an astonishing piece of work which takes fifty years to complete. Exclaim, when you see one: 'It's more beautiful than any painting!' The tapestry-worker has no idea what he is making.

GODDAM 'The backbone of the English language,' as Beaumarchais remarked. Laugh superciliously as you say it.

GODFATHER Always the child's real father.

GOG Always comes with Magog.

GORDIAN KNOT Something to do with antiquity. The way the Greeks knotted their ties.

GOSPELS Divine, sublime, etc.

GOTHIC Style of architecture known to excite religious feelings more effectively than any other.

GRAMMAR Teach it to even the youngest children, as something easy and simple.

GRAMMARIANS All pedants.

GREEK Anything you don't understand, it's all Greek.

GROG Not a respectable drink.

GROTTO WITH STALACTITES Splendid festivities in there, many years ago, a ball or a banquet, given by somebody important. You can see stalactites that 'look like organ pipes'. Mass was said there, clandestinely, during the Revolution.

GUERRILLAS Do the enemy more damage than the regular army.

GUESTS Quote their behaviour as an example to your son.

GULF-STREAM Famous town in Norway, recently discovered.

GYMNASTICS Impossible to do enough. Exhausting for children.

H

HABIT Be sure to add: 'It's second nature.' School-boy habits are always undesirable. Anyone can play the violin like Paganini, it's just a question of habit.

HACK Word for *journalist*. To be especially insulting, add 'mercenary'.

HAEMORRHOIDS Come from sitting on stone benches and on hot stoves. St Fiacre's disease. Haemorrhoids are a sign of good health, do not attempt to treat them.

HAM Always comes from Mainz. Beware of the risk of trichinosis.

HAMMOCK Creole women are especially fond of them. Essential item in any garden. Convince yourself it's more comfortable than a bed.

HAND To have a fine hand means to have beautiful handwriting.

HARD Without exception, add the phrase 'as iron'. There is of course 'hard as a rock', but it's less emphatic.

HAREM Always compare a cock and his hens to a sultan in a harem. Every schoolboy's dream.

HARES Sleep with their eyes open.

HARP Produces celestial harmonies. In old prints, played only among ruins or beside a mountain torrent. Shows off the arm and the hand.

HAT Complain about the shape of hats.

HEALTH In excess, a cause of illness.

HEAT Always unbearable. Don't drink in hot weather.

HELOTS Hold them up as an example to your son, though they are rather difficult to find.

HERMAPHRODITES Excite an unhealthy curiosity. Try to see one.

HERNIA Everybody has one, without realizing.

HERRINGS Source of Holland's wealth. (Quote what Casanova said about them.)

HIATUS Not to be tolerated.

HICCUPS Cured by putting a key down the back, or by a fright.

HIEROGLYPHICS Ancient Egyptian language, devised by the priests to conceal their nefarious secrets. And to think that there are people who can decipher them! Anyway, it might be just a hoax!

HOMER Never existed. Famous for his laugh. 'Homeric laughter'.

HOMO Say '*Ecce homo!*' when you see someone you've been waiting for.

HORN, HUNTING Sounds impressive in the woods, and across water at night.

HORSE If they knew their own strength, they would not let themselves be led. Horsemeat: good subject for a pamphlet by a man who wants to launch himself as an important public figure. Racehorses: scoff at them. What use are they?

HOSTILITY Hostilities are like oysters, you open them. 'Hostilities have been opened.' It sounds like an invitation to come and sit at the table.

HOTELS Are only decent in Switzerland.

HOUSE, ON FIRE Sight worth seeing.

HUGO, VICTOR Made a very great mistake indeed, getting involved in politics.

HUMIDITY Cause of all illnesses.

HUNCHBACK Refer to it as 'a gibbosity', it's more

polite. Touching the hunch brings good luck. Are very witty. Greatly prized by lascivious women.

HUNTSMEN Always telling tall stories. Call them 'Nimrod', they always find it flattering, without knowing why. Alternatively, call them 'Great hunters in the face of the Lord'. Hunting paraphernalia. You get up early . . . The footwear, hefty in proportion to the distance to be covered. Huntsmen fake a countrified air.

HUSSAR Pronounced 'huzzar'. Always preceded by 'noble' or 'dashing'. The ladies adore them. Never miss the opportunity to quote: 'Thou who dost know the hussars of the guard . . .'

HYDRA The hydra of anarchism, the hydra of socialism, and so on for all doctrines that cause any alarm. Try to vanquish them.

HYDROTHERAPY Can cure anything, and also cause it.

HYGIENE Must always be 'carefully maintained'. Prevents illness, except when it causes it.

HYPOTHESIS Often 'dangerous', always 'daring'.

HYSTERIA Confuse with nymphomania. Current notions of hysteria. A hysterical woman is every pervert's dream.

I

ICE-CREAM Dangerous thing to eat.

ICE-CREAM SELLERS All come from Naples.

IDEALS Completely useless.

IDEOLOGUE All journalists are ideologues.

IDLERS All Parisians are idlers even though ninety per cent of the inhabitants of Paris come from the provinces. In Paris, no one does any work.

IDOLATERS Are cannibals.

ILIAD Always followed by *The Odyssey*.

ILLEGIBLE A doctor's prescription ought to be illegible. So should any official signature. Private signatures likewise. Shows that you are overwhelmingly busy.

ILLUSIONS Pretend to have a whole host. Lament the fact that you've lost them.

IMAGES There are always too many in a poem.

IMAGINATION Always 'lively'. Be on your guard against it. If you haven't any yourself, denigrate it in others. To write novels, all you need is imagination.

IMBECILE Anyone who thinks differently from you.

IMMORALITY If uttered vehemently, this word will

greatly enhance the standing of the speaker.

IMPERIALISTS All respectable, polite, peaceable, genteel people.

IMPIETY Denounce loudly.

IMPORTS The worm in the bud of commerce.

IMPRESARIO Artist's word, means 'manager'. Always preceded by 'brilliant'.

INAUGURATION Joyful occasion.

INCOGNITO What princes wear on their travels.

INCOMPETENCE Always 'total'. The more incompetent you are, the more ambitious you must be.

INDIARUBBER Made from a horse's scrotum.

INDOLENCE Caused by warm climates.

INDUSTRY Splendid career. Endless possibilities. More aristocratic than commerce. Aristotle was a perfume-maker in Athens. (See *commerce*.)

INFANTICIDE Committed only among the working classes.

INFINITESIMAL No idea what it means, but it's connected with homeopathy.

INFORMERS All work for the police.

INKWELL Present suitable for a doctor.

INNOVATION Always 'dangerous'.

INQUISITION Its crimes have been much exaggerated.

INSCRIPTION Always cuneiform.

INSPIRATION, POETIC Things that set it off: the sight of the sea, love, women, etc.

INSTITUTE, THE All the members of The Institute are old men with green taffeta eye-shades.[7]

INSTRUMENT An instrument that has been used to commit a crime is always 'blunt', unless it's actually 'sharp'.

INSURRECTION 'Our most sacred duty' (Blanqui).

INTEGRITY Found especially among the judiciary.

INTERVAL Always too long.

INTRIGUE Can unlock any door. Only way to get on.

INTRODUCTION Obscene word.

INVASION Excites tears.

INVENTORS Always die in the work-house. Someone else profits from their discovery, it's so unfair.

IRON To govern France requires an iron hand.

ITALY Should be visited immediately after the wedding ceremony. Endlessly disappointing, not as beautiful as they say.

IVORY Word applied only to teeth.

---

[7] The Institute: *L'Institut de France*, a learned society incorporating the five official Academies.

J

JAPAN Everything there is made of porcelain.

JASPER All the vases in museums are made of jasper.

JAVELIN As good as any gun, if you know how to use it.

JE NE SAIS QUOI When looking at a statue, always say: 'It has a certain *je ne sais quoi*.'

JOCKEY-CLUB Its members are all bright young things with lots of money. Refer to it simply as 'The Jockey'; this is very chic, people will think you are a member.

JOHN BULL When you don't know an Englishman's name, call him John Bull.

JOURNEY Get it over with as quickly as possible.

JURY Do your best to avoid being on one.

JUSTICE Never give it a thought.

K

KALEIDOSCOPE Only to be used when describing an exhibition of paintings.

KEEPSAKE Always have one on the table in your drawing-room.

KISS Say 'embrace', more decent. Stolen kisses sweetest. The kiss is placed on a girl's brow, a mother's cheek, a pretty woman's hand, a child's neck, a mistress's lips.

KNAPSACK Carrying-case for a field-marshal's baton.

KNIFE Catalonian if the blade is long; called a dagger if it has been used to commit a crime.

KORAN Book by Mohammed, exclusively about women.

L

LABORATORY Good idea to have one if you live in the country.

LACONIC A dead language.

LADIES Ladies first. The ladies, God bless them all. Never say: 'Those ladies are in the drawing-room'.[8]

LAFAYETTE A general, famous for his white horse.

LAGOON City on the Adriatic.

---

[8] Because the phrase 'those ladies' was a facetious masculine euphemism for prostitutes.

LAKE Always have a woman by your side when you go out sailing on a lake.

LAMPOON A lost art.

LANDLORD The human race is divided into two great classes: landlords and tenants. 'What is your profession? – Landlord.'

LANDSCAPE PAINTINGS Always look like 'a plate of spinach'.

LATHE Essential item to have up in the attic when you live in the country, for use on wet days.

LATIN Man's natural language. Spoils your style. Useful only for reading the inscriptions on public fountains. Beware of quotations in Latin: they always conceal something improper.

LAUGHTER Always Homeric.

LAUREL Laurels prevent you from sleeping.

LAW Governments that mean to govern always have to bend the law. Rules and regulations will be the death of us.

LAW, THE No one knows what it is.

LAXATIVE Taken in secret.

LEAGUE You can travel a league more quickly than you can go four kilometres.

LEARNING, MEN OF Disparage them. Erudition is just a matter of memory and hard work. Knowledge: sublime infusion. A walking encyclopedia.

LEATHER All leather comes from Russia.

LEFT-HANDERS Tremendous at fencing. More deft than people who are right-handed.

LEGION OF HONOUR, MEDAL OF THE To be sneered at, even though you rather covet one. When you eventually get it, always say it came quite unsolicited.

LENT Basically a simple health measure.

LETHARGY Sometimes it can last for years.

LIBERTINISM Found only in big cities.

LIBERTY 'Liberty, what crimes are committed in thy name!' We have all the liberties that we need. 'Liberty is not licence.' Conservative sayings.

LIBRARY Always have one at home, particularly if you live in the country.

LICKSPITTLE Weighty insult in the grand style, to be hurled at one's political opponents. 'Sir! You are merely a lickspittle in thrall to the clique in the Elysée!' Used only from the rostrum.

LIGHT Always say, '*Fiat lux*,' when anyone lights a candle.

LILAC Delightful: it means that summer is coming.

LION Noble creature. Always playing with a ball. Well roared, lion! To think that lions and tigers are only cats.

LION-TAMERS Use obscene methods.

LITERATURE An occupation for idlers.

LOBSTER A giant prawn.

LOCKET Should always contain a lock of hair or a photograph.

LORD Rich Englishman.

LUXURY The undoing of many an empire.

LYNX Animal famous for its eyes.

M

MACADAM Has done away with revolutions: it leaves nothing to build barricades with. Most inconvenient, for all that.

MACARONI Served with the fingers, when eaten Italian style.

MACHIAVELLIAN The word should always be spoken with a shudder.

MACKINTOSH Scottish philosopher. Inventor of the raincoat.

MAESTRO Italian word meaning 'pianist'.

MAGISTRATE Splendid career for a young man. Magistrates are all pederasts.

MAGNETISM Excellent topic of conversation, with opportunities for flirtation.

MAID Use the word only when referring to Joan of Arc, as in the phrase 'The Maid of Orléans'.

MAIDS All incompetent. Servants are so hard to find these days!

MAJOLICA Smarter than porcelain.

MALACCA Walking-sticks should be made of malacca.

MALEDICTION Always proclaimed by a father.

MALTHUS 'The infamous!' No need to know even the title of his book.

MANDOLIN Indispensable for seducing Spanish women.

MARBLE All statues are made of Parian marble.

MARINER Always 'intrepid'.

MARTYRS All the early Christians were.

MASK Makes you witty.

MATRIX Synonym for vulva.

MASTURBATION 'Self-pollution that thwarts the intentions of nature, usually with the very direst consequences.'[9]

MATERIALISM Utter the word in a horrified tone, emphasizing every syllable.

MATHEMATICS Desiccates the heart.

[9] Alphabetical order has been teasingly 'disturbed' by the inversion of *matrix* and *masturbation*. At this point the French text refers the reader to the entry in the contemporary *Dictionnaire d'Académie*.

MATTRESS The harder it is the healthier it is.

MAY-BUGS Heralds of summer. Splendid subject for a short monograph. Their total destruction is the dream of every prefect. In a speech at an agricultural show, when describing the devastation they cause, refer to them as 'accursed coleoptera'.

MECHANICS Lower branch of mathematics.

MEDALS Made only in antiquity.

MEDICAL STUDENTS Sleep next to corpses. Some are known to eat them.

MEDICINE Jeer at it when in good health.

MELANCHOLY Sign of a noble heart and a lofty spirit.

MELODRAMA Less immoral than drama.

MELON Nice topic for dinner-table conversation. Is it a vegetable? Is it a fruit? The English eat it as a dessert, which is astounding.

MEMORY Insist that your memory is deplorable; you may even boast that you have none at all. But bellow with rage if anyone says you have no judgement.

MEPHISTOPHELIAN All bitter laughter should be described as Mephistophelian.

MERCURY Finishes off the patient along with the disease.

METALLURGY Very chic.

METAMORPHOSIS Laugh at the fact that people once believed in it. Ovid invented the whole thing.

METAPHORS Writers always use too many of them!

METAPHYSICS No need to know what it is. Laugh at it: this creates an impression of great intelligence.

METHOD Completely useless.

MIDNIGHT Marks the limit of honest toil and innocent pleasure. Beyond midnight, all activities are immoral.

MIGHT 'Might makes Right' (Bismarck).

MILK Dissolves oysters. Attracts snakes. Whitens the skin. Certain women in Paris bathe in milk every morning.

MINISTER OF STATE Summit of human achievement.

MINUTE No one realizes how long a minute can be.

MISSIONARIES All get eaten or crucified.

MISSIVE More prestigious than a *letter*.

MODESTY A woman's greatest charm.

MOLE 'Blind as a mole.' Yet they do actually have eyes.

MONARCHY A constitutional monarchy is the best of republics.

MONEY Root of all evil. Say: '*Auri sacra fames.*' The

god of the day (not to be confused with Apollo). Government ministers have a remuneration; lawyers draw emoluments; doctors have fees; employees receive a salary, workers get paid, servants are given wages. Money doesn't make you happy.

MONK Knight of Onan.

MONKEY Never forget to add: son of the monk. This joke is always a great success.

MONOPOLIES, GOVERNMENT Denounce loudly.

MONSTERS You never see any these days.

MOON Inspires melancholy. Possibly inhabited?

MORTGAGE Demand 'the reform of the entire mortgage system'. Very stylish.

MOSAIC The secret has been lost.

MOSQUITO More dangerous than any wild animal.

MOUSTACHE Gives a military air.

MUSHROOMS Only eat the ones they sell in the market.

MUSIC Makes one think of all kinds of things. Has a beneficial effect on public life. The *Marseillaise* for instance.

MUSICIAN The mark of a true musician is to compose no music at all, to play no instrument and to despise all virtuosi.

MUSSELS Always cause indigestion.

MUSTARD You can only get decent mustard in Dijon. Ruins your stomach eventually.

N

NAPLES 'See Naples and die!' (See *Seville*.) If you are talking to a learned man refer to it as Parthenopeia.

NATIONS Advocate union of all races.

NECKERCHIEF Very *comme il faut* to blow your nose in it.

NECTAR Confuse it with ambrosia.

NEGRESSES Randier than white women. (See *brunettes* and *blondes*.)

NEGROES Remark in a surprised tone that their saliva is white and they can speak French.

NERVES Invoke them whenever faced by a baffling illness: 'It's your nerves!' This explanation satisfies everyone.

NERVOUS AILMENT Always a sham.

NEWSPAPERS Impossible to do without them, but denounce them loudly all the same. Their importance in modern society. Example: *Le Figaro*. Serious journals: *Revue des Deux Mondes*, *L'Economiste*, *Le Journal des Débats*. Leave them out on the table in your drawing-room, making sure you cut the pages beforehand. Mark a few passages in red pencil, it makes an excellent impression. In the morning read an article in one of these sage and serious journals. Then in the evening, when you have guests, steer the conversation deftly towards the topic which you have been reading about. This is your opportunity to sparkle.

NICE Word for anything agreeable. 'That's really nice!' expresses the very peak of admiration.

NIGHTMARES Caused by indigestion.

NOSTRILS Flared nostrils, sign of lubricity.

NOVELS Pervert the masses. Less immoral in serial form than when published in hardback. Only historical novels ought to be allowed, because they teach history. *The Three Musketeers* for instance. Some novels are written with the tip of a scalpel (*Madame Bovary*, for example). Some are built on the point of a needle.

O

OASIS A tavern in the desert.

OBESITY Causes of . . .

OBSCENITY All the scientific words derived from Greek and Latin conceal some obscenity.

OCEAN Image of the infinite.

OCTOGENARIAN Applied to any elderly person.

ODALISQUES All women in the Orient are odalisques. (See *dancing-girls*.)

OFFICIALS Inspire respect, whatever office they perform.

OLD MEN After a flood or a thunderstorm, or whatever, the old men in the village will always say that they cannot remember ever seeing anything like it.

OLIVE OIL Never any good. You need to have a friend in Marseilles who can send you little casks of the real thing.

OMEGA Second letter of the Greek alphabet, hence the phrase 'the alpha and the omega'.

OPERA (BACKSTAGE) Mohammed's earthly paradise.

OPTIMIST Synonym for 'imbecile'.

ORCHESTRA Image of society: everyone plays their part and there's someone in charge.

ORCHITIS Gentleman's ailment.

ORDER 'What crimes are committed in thy name!' (See *liberty*.)

ORGAN Raises the soul towards God.

ORIENTALIST Man who has travelled extensively.

ORIGINALITY Jeer at it, you will be thought a most superior person. Express scorn and hatred for all forms of originality; exterminate it if you can.

OTTER Their fur is useful for making hats and waistcoats.

OUTRAGE Subject to the worst form of outrage.

OYSTERS Nobody eats them, these days! They're too expensive!

P

PAGANINI Never tuned his violin. Had amazingly long fingers.

PALFREY White creature known in medieval times, but now totally extinct.

PALM TREE Provides local colour.

PALMYRA An Egyptian Queen? Or an ancient monument? Nobody knows.

PANTHEISM Absurdity. Denounce loudly.

PARADOX Always coined on the Boulevard des Italiens, while puffing on a cigarette.

PARALLELS You are allowed to choose from amongst the following. Caesar and Pompey, Horace and Virgil, Voltaire and Rousseau,

Napoleon and Charlemagne, Goethe and Schiller, Bayard and MacMahon.

PARIS The great whore. The Capital. Provincial view of (and vice versa). Heaven for women, hell for horses.

PARTS Some people have shameful parts, to others they are quite natural.

PASSPORT A pleasant smile is the best passport of all.

PEBBLES On a beach, always collect pebbles to take home.

PEDANTRY Scoff at it, except when it is brought to bear on something utterly trivial.

PEDERASTY All men are afflicted by this malady at a certain age.

PELICAN Pecks its breast open to feed its young. Emblem of the *paterfamilias*.

PERSPIRATION Smelly feet. Sign of good health.

PHAETON Inventor of the carriage of the same name.

PHEASANT Very smart to have it at dinner parties.

PHILOSOPHY Always jeer at it.

PHLEGM Always described as 'imperturbable'. Try to be phlegmatic; it shows style and it looks very English.

PHOENIX Splendid name for any Fire Insurance Company.

PHOTOGRAPHY Will take the place of painting. (See *daguerrotype*.)

PIANO Indispensable in a drawing-room.

PIGEON Should only ever be eaten with peas.

PIGS Their innards being 'just the same as a man's', they ought to be used in hospitals to teach anatomy.

PIKESTAFF You must surely be able to see it.

PILLOW Avoid using a pillow, it can turn you into a hunchback.

PIMPLES On the face or elsewhere, sign of healthy, strong blood. Never squeeze them.

PINCE-NEZ Insolent and distinguished.

PIPE Bad form, except at the seaside.

PLANTS Always cure the part of the human body which they resemble.

PLEASURE The mother of fun and games; don't mention her 'daughters'.

PLUMPNESS Sign of wealth and idleness. Sleeping after dinner. Beer.

POACHERS All ex-convicts. Responsible for all crimes committed in rural areas. Opportunity for display of frenzied rage: 'Punishment, my dear sir, ruthless punishment!'

POCK-MARKS Pock-marked women are always lascivious.

POET Lofty synonym for 'blockhead'; dreamer.

POETRY Completely useless, unfashionable.

POLICE Always in the wrong.

POLICE, THE Refer to them as 'the officers of the law' or 'the constabulary'.

POLICEMAN Bastion of society.

POLITICAL ECONOMY Heartless science.

PORTFOLIO Carrying one under your arm will make you look like a government minister.

PORTRAIT The problem is to paint the smile.

PRACTICAL JOKES Highly recommended when picnicking with ladies.

PRACTICE Superior to theory.

PRAGMATIC SANCTION No one knows what it is.

PRESENTS, CHRISTMAS Express indignation at.

PRIAPISM Classical religion.

PRIESTHOOD Art is a priesthood. So are medicine, journalism, law, and all professions in general.

PRIESTS Ought to be castrated. Sleep with their servant-girls and beget children that they call their 'nephews'. 'All the same, there are a few decent ones.'

PRINCIPLES Always incontestable. Impossible to state either the nature or the number of one's principles. No matter. They are sacred.

PRINT Believe whatever you see in print. Ah, to

have your name in print! There are certain people who commit a crime for that pleasure alone.

PROFESSOR Always erudite.

PROGRESS Always ill-conceived and over-hasty.

PROPELLER Machine of the future.

PROPERTY One of the very foundations of society. More sacred than religion.

PROSE Easier to write than poetry.

PROSTITUTE A necessary evil. Protection for our daughters and our sisters, as long as there are unmarried men. Should be hounded relentlessly. It is no longer possible to walk the street with one's wife unmolested. Are always daughters of the people seduced by bourgeois men.

PRUNES Prunes unblock your bowels.

PUDDING It wouldn't be Christmas without the pudding.

PUNCH Suitable drink for an evening with the boys. Source of great hilarity. Put out the light when you set fire to it. It produces 'the most amazing flames'.

PYRAMID Useless edifice.

Q

QUESTION To pose it is to resolve it.

R

RABBIT STEW Always made with cats.

RACINE Pervert!

RADICALISM All the more dangerous in its latent form. The republic is leading us down the road to radicalism.

RAILWAY STATIONS Go into raptures and declare them the very pattern of architecture.

RAILWAYS If Napoleon had had them, he would have been invincible. Rhapsodize over what they have accomplished, saying: 'My dear sir, I who am speaking to you here, this morning I was in X, I went on the train to Y, I attended to my business there, and here I am back again.'

RAINCOAT Most becoming garment. Very detrimental because it traps perspiration.

RAPTURE Obscene word.

RECONCILIATION Always advocate it, even when both parties are implacable.

RED-HEADS See *blondes*, *brunettes* and *negresses*.

REGENCY Endless suppers.

RELATIVES Always a problem. Unless they're rich, keep them out of sight.

RELIGION One of the foundations of society. Necessary for the masses, but let there not be too much of it. 'The religion of our fathers': say it in a smoothly obsequious tone.

REPUBLICANS Republicans are not all thieves, but all thieves are republicans.

RESTAURANT Always order the things you rarely eat at home. When perplexed, simply order whatever they are having on the next table.

REVOLUTION, AGE OF Must be still in progress, because every government promises to put an end to it.

RHYME Never accords with reason.

RING It is very distinguished to wear one on the index finger. Putting one on the thumb is too oriental. Wearing rings deforms the fingers.

ROBE Inspires respect.

ROCK BOTTOM Excellent name for a shop, inspires confidence.

RONSARD Ridiculous, with all his Greek and Latin words.

ROPE People don't realize how strong a rope is. More solid than iron.

RUINS Encourage reverie and add a certain poetry to the landscape.

S

SABRE The French want to be governed by a sabre.

SACRILEGE It is a sacrilege to cut down a tree.

SAFES Actually very easy to crack.

SAINT BARTHOLOMEW'S DAY MASSACRE A load of old nonsense.

SAINT HELENA Island famous for its cliffs.

SALON A Salon review is an excellent way to make a literary debut: it displays a man's talents to the full.

SALT-CELLAR Knocking over the salt-cellar brings bad luck.

SANITATION Bleach, carbolic acid.

SAPHICS AND ADONICS Mention them in a critical essay. The effect is most impressive.

SASH Poetic.

SATRAP Rich debauchee.

SATURNALIA Revolutionary festivals held in the late 1790s.

SCAFFOLD When you mount the scaffold, arrange to say something eloquent before you die.

SCHOOL TEACHERS (FEMALE) Always come from good families down on their luck. Dangerous to have them in the house, usually corrupt the husband. Should always be exceedingly ugly.

SCOTS, MARY QUEEN OF Pity her fate.

SCUDÉRY Poke fun, without being sure if he was a man or a woman.

SEA Bottomless. Image of the infinite. Inspires great thoughts. At the seaside you should always carry a telescope. When you gaze at the sea, always say: 'What a lot of water!'

SEA-SICKNESS To avoid getting it, simply think of something else.

SEALED Always 'hermetically'.

SECRETIONS Be delighted when they appear and express amazement that the human body can contain such quantities of fluid.

SEIGNEUR, DROIT DE Profess not to believe in it.

SELLING Buying and selling, what life is for.

SERVANTS All thieves.

SEVILLE Famous for its barber. See Seville and die. (See *Naples*.)

SHELLS, ARTILLERY Useful for making clocks and inkwells.

SHEPHERDS All shepherds are sorcerers. Their speciality is conversation with the Virgin Mary.

SHOTGUN Always have one handy in the country.

SIGH Heave it when a woman is near.

SIGNATURE The more ornate you can make it, the finer it is.

SINECURE Always be on the lookout for one.

SINGERS Swallow a raw egg every morning to brighten up their voices. A tenor voice is always tender and charming, a baritone is rich and pleasing, and a bass is a powerful organ.

SKIRT, BIT OF Impossible to find, these days. Say it with the disconsolate air of a keen sportsman lamenting the absence of game.

SLEEP Too much sleep thickens the blood.

SLUMS Terrible in times of revolution.

SMOKING-CAP Indispensable accessory for the scholar. Lends great dignity to the face.

SNAKES All poisonous.

SNEEZING After saying 'Bless you,' embark on a discussion of the origin of this custom. It is witty to say that Russian and Polish are not spoken, they are sneezed. Every time you sneeze, you have to say: 'I must be getting a cold.'

SNIPERS More terrifying than the enemy.

SNUFF Men of learning usually take it. If you take

snuff people will think you are a doctor. (See *tobacco*.)

SOCIETY Its enemies. What causes its destruction.

SOIL, THE Refer to the soil in a mournful tone.

SOLICITORS Not to be trusted, these days.

SOMNAMBULISTS Walk across the rooftops in the night.

SON-IN-LAW 'My dear boy, we're broke!'

SOUTHERN COOKING Full of garlic. Disparage it vociferously.

SOUTHERNERS All poets.

SPICE Plural of spouse. (*Old-fashioned*, but still gets a laugh.)

SPINACH Sweeps out your stomach like a broom. Never fail to quote Prudhomme's famous remark: 'I don't like it, and I'm glad I don't, because if I did then I'd eat it, and I can't stand it.' (Some people will find this all perfectly logical and won't laugh.)

SPIRITUALISM The best system of philosophy.

SPONTANEOUS GENERATION Socialist notion.

SPRING Have yourself bled in the spring.

SPURS Look nice on a pair of boots.

SPY Always upper-class. (See *swindler*.)

SQUARING THE CIRCLE No one knows what it

means, but you are supposed to shrug your shoulders when it's mentioned.

SQUIREARCHY Declare one's supreme contempt for it.

STAG PARTY Calls for oysters, white wine and smutty jokes.

STAGE SCENERY Not proper painting: you simply hurl a bucket of paint at the canvas; then you spread it with a broom; all the rest is just a matter of distance and lighting.

STAINED GLASS The secret is lost.

STALLION Always lunging. A woman ought not to know the difference between a stallion and a horse. A little girl can be told that a stallion is merely a large horse.

STAR Follow your star, as Napoleon did.

STEADY Always 'as a rock'.

STOCK EXCHANGE Barometer of public opinion.

STOCKBROKERS All thieves.

STOICISM Is impossible.

STOMACH All illnesses come from the stomach.

STROLL Always take a stroll after dinner: it's good for your digestion.

STUD-FARMS Excellent subject for a parliamentary debate.

STUDENTS All wear red berets and tight cavalry-style trousers, smoke pipes in the street and never do any work.

SUCCESS When referring to a successful man, say that he is 'fortune's minion'. No one knows what it means, and neither will your listener.

SUICIDE Sign of cowardice.

SUMMER Always exceptional. (See *winter*.)

SUMMER-HOUSE Temple of delight in the garden.

SUNDAYS Tell the story of the oxen that wouldn't work on Sundays.

SUPPER Regency supper: flowers, candlelight, women half-naked, etc. The wit flowed faster than the champagne.

SURGEONS Hard-hearted: refer to them as butchers.

SWALLOWS Always refer to them as 'harbingers of spring'. Since no one knows where they come from, you can say that they are 'travellers from a distant shore'. This is poetic.

SWAN Sings before it dies. Can break a man's leg with its wing. The Swan of Avon was not a bird but a man called Shakespeare. The Swan of Mantua means Virgil. The Swan of Pesaro means Rossini.

SWINDLER Always upper-class. (See *spy*.)

SYBARITES Denounce loudly.

SYPHILIS Everyone, more or less, is affected by it.

T

TASK Always 'Herculean'.

TASTE Simplicity is the secret of good taste. Should always be said to a woman who apologizes for the ordinariness of her dress.

TEENAGER Always begin a school prize-day speech with the phrase 'You young teenagers . . .', which is a tautology.

TEETH Damaged by cider, tobacco, sweets, ices, drinking straight after soup and sleeping with the mouth open. *Eye-teeth*: dangerous having them extracted because they're linked to the eyes. Having a tooth out is 'no laughing matter'.

TEN, COUNCIL OF Nobody knows what it was, but it was dreadful. Wore masks at their meetings. Still shudder at the thought.

THICKET Always describe it as 'dark and impenetrable'.

THINKING Painful; things that make us think are generally neglected.

THIRTEEN Avoid being thirteen at the table, it brings bad luck. The strong-minded should always make the following remark: 'Never mind,

I'll eat enough for two.' Or else, if there are ladies present, ask if anyone is pregnant.

THUGS Word used by hard-line republicans to designate the police force.

THUNDERBOLTS FROM THE VATICAN Laugh at them.

TIGHTS Very exciting.

TOAD Male frog. Carries a highly dangerous poison. Lives inside stones.

TOBACCO The stuff they sell in the shops is not as good as contraband tobacco. Cause of all the ailments that affect the brain and the spinal cord.

TOLLS Evading them is no crime. It's a sign of sophistication and political independence.

TOYS Should always be educational.

TRAVELLER Always 'intrepid'. 'There you are, you intrepid traveller.' Always preceded by 'gentlemen', railway-notice style: 'Gentlemen travellers . . .'

TROUBADOUR Splendid subject for an ornamental clock.

TRUFFLES Abstain from eating them when your wife is unwell.

U

UNIVERSAL SUFFRAGE Zenith of political science.
UNIVERSITY *Alma mater.*
UNLEASH You unleash dogs and wicked passions.

V

VACCINE Don't mix with people who haven't been
vaccinated.
VELVET On lapels, sign of distinction and wealth.
VILE 'It is utterly vile!' Any work of art or literature
which *Le Figaro* does not endorse.
VOLTAIRE Best known for his terrible 'rictus'. A
shallow intellect.

W

WAGNER Sneer when you hear his name, and make
jokes about the music of the future.
WALLS, WITHIN THESE Good phrase to use in any
official speech: 'Gentlemen, within these very
walls . . .'

WALTZ Deplore it vociferously. Lascivious and impure dance which should only be danced by old women.

WAR Denounce fiercely.

WATCH The only decent ones are made in Geneva. In a pantomime, whenever a character pulls out his watch, it has to be an onion. This joke never fails. 'Does your watch keep good time?' 'You can set the sun by it.'

WATER The water in Paris gives you colic. Sea water holds you up when you swim. Cologne water smells nice.

WAX-POLISHING Only effective if you do it yourself.

WHATNOT Essential item in an attractive woman's sitting-room.

WHIMSY It is quite proper to describe any lofty ideas which you don't understand as 'mere whimsy'.

WINDMILL Looks nice in a landscape.

WINE Topic of masculine conversation. Bordeaux wines are best, because doctors prescribe them. The worse they taste the more natural they are.

WINTER Always exceptional. (See *summer*.) Healthier than any other season.

WINTER EVENINGS In the country they are spent decorously.

WIT Always sparkling. Brevity the soul of. Great wits are to madness near allied.

WITNESS Always refuse to be a witness in a court-case, because you never know where it might end up.

WOMAN Person of the fair sex. Things suitable for a woman. Importance of women today. Do not say 'my wife', say 'my spouse', or preferably 'my better half'.

WOMEN'S CLOTHES Trouble the imagination.

WOODS Inspire reverie. (See *beauty spots*.) When out walking in the autumn always say: 'The woods decay, the woods decay and fall . . .'

WORKER Always honest and obliging, when he's not on the barricades.

WRITING Put 'Yours in haste' at the end, a good excuse for spelling mistakes and a clumsy style. Handwriting: good handwriting opens every door. Indecipherable: sign of knowledge, for example, doctors' prescriptions.

WRITTEN, WELL-WRITTEN Porter's phrase, to describe the pulp-fiction he most enjoys.

Y

YAWNING Always say: 'Do excuse me, it's not boredom, it's just my stomach.'

YOUNG GENTLEMEN Always up to mischief, scarcely proper for them to be any other way. 'Good grief! And you a young man!' Appropriate exploits include: singing, blaspheming, running up debts (in moderation though).

YOUNG LADY Speak the phrase bashfully. All young ladies are pale, fragile and invariably pure. They should be kept away from books of all kinds, and forbidden to visit museums and theatres. The monkey-house at the zoo is particularly to be avoided.

YOURS Always 'in haste'.

YOUTH Ah, what a splendid thing it is! Always quote this Italian poem, even though you have no idea what it means: *O Primavera! Gioventu dell'-anno! O Gioventu! Primavera della vita!*